VEHICLES

ADVENTURES IN STEAM

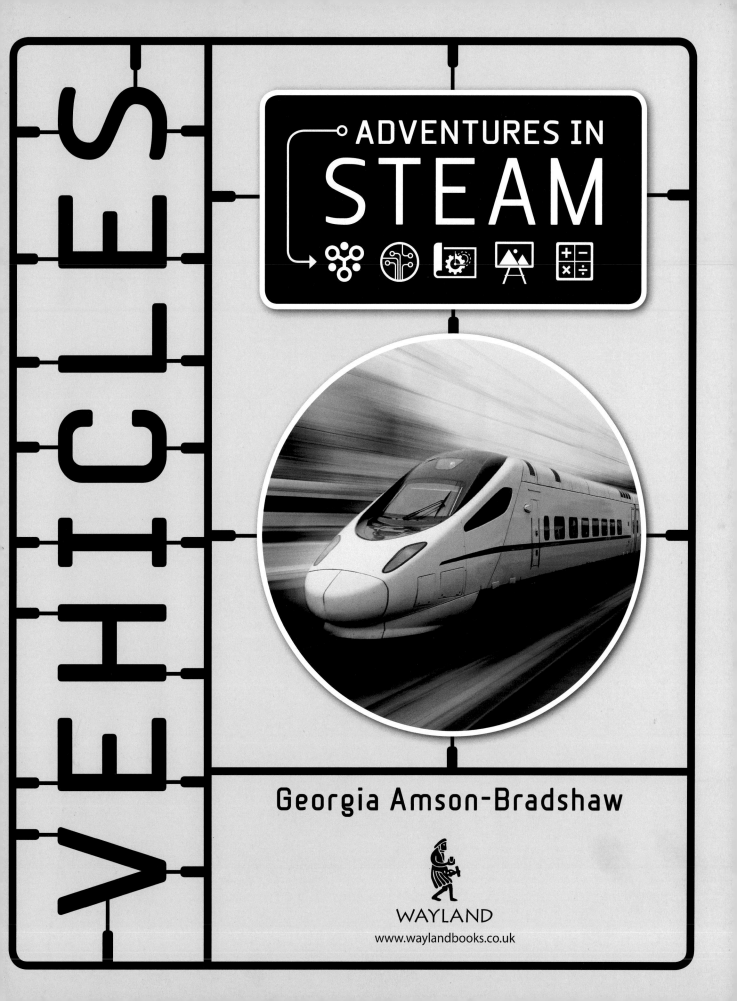

Georgia Amson-Bradshaw

WAYLAND
www.waylandbooks.co.uk

First published in Great Britain in 2017 by Wayland

Series editor: Izzi Howell
Designer: Rocket Design (East Anglia) Ltd
Illustrations: Rocket Design (East Anglia) Ltd and Julian Baker
In-house editor: Julia Bird/Catherine Brereton

ISBN: 978 1 5263 0481 0
10 9 8 7 6 5 4 3 2 1

MIX
Paper from
responsible sources
FSC
www.fsc.org
FSC® C104740

Wayland
An imprint of
Hachette Children's Group
Part of Hodder & Stoughton
Carmelite House
50 Victoria Embankment
London EC4Y 0DZ

An Hachette UK Company
www.hachette.co.uk
www.hachettechildrens.co.uk

Printed in China

Picture acknowledgements:
Images from Shutterstock.com: NelliGal 4c, galimovma79 4b, poramet panjaroen 5t, Bildagentur Zoonar
GmbH 7t, NarayTrace 7br, XL1200 8tr, Ljupco Smokovski 9tr, ilozavr 10bl, Everett Collection 11c, Perry
Correll 11br, Whitevector 12t, Arak Rattanawijittakorn 13t, Ortodox 16t, Everett Historical 16b, cyo
bo 17t, Designua 18br, Yauheni Meshcharakou 20t, Aun Photographer 21t, Arak Rattanawijittakorn 21br,
photowind 22c, Photo_mts 23br, NeonLight 24l, Everett Historical 25b, Digital Storm 26l, Verticalarray 27t, Szekretar
Zsolt 28t, shaineast 29t, Nikita Chisnikov 30tr, Wildeside 30b, Nerthuz 31t, iurii 31b, wassiliy-architect 32b,
ktsdesign 34c, vrx 34b, grynold 35b, kpakook 36t, Mehdi Photos 37t, Action Sports Photography 37b, Dmitry
Kalinovsky 38bl, conrado 39t, Graphic Compressor 39br, Kevin M. McCarthy 40t, Travel Bug 41r, Mikhail
Bakunovich 41br, Martial Red 45t, Patrick Breig 45b

All design elements from Shutterstock.

CONTENTS

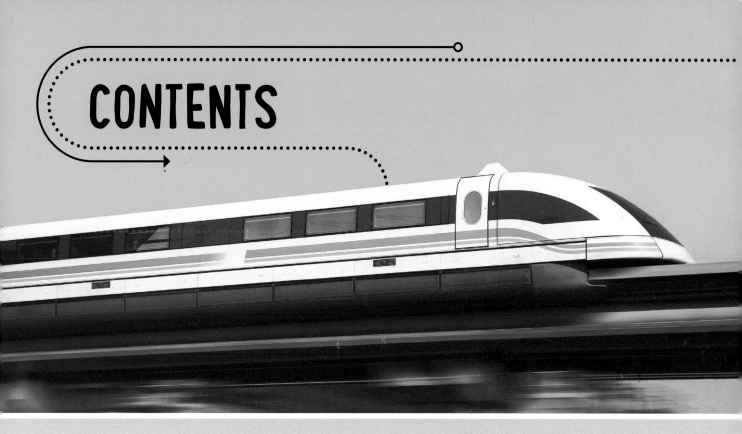

DESIGNING A VEHICLE

A VEHICLE IS A MOBILE MACHINE FOR TRANSPORTING PEOPLE OR THINGS. PEOPLE HAVE USED VEHICLES FOR THOUSANDS OF YEARS. WE NEED THEM FOR WORK AND LEISURE, TO TRANSPORT OURSELVES AND TO MOVE GOODS AROUND THE WORLD. THEY RANGE IN SIZE AND COMPLEXITY FROM A SIMPLE PUSH SCOOTER TO CRUISE SHIPS WITH THOUSANDS OF PASSENGERS.

When designing a vehicle, there are lots of factors to consider. What terrain will the vehicle need to cover? Will the vehicle travel over land, water or through the air? Will the vehicle mainly transport people or goods? Is the capacity or the speed of the vehicle the priority?

Mining trucks are designed to cover rough terrain carrying heavy loads.

SCIENCE TALK

Designing an efficient vehicle requires a good understanding of the forces that act on a moving vehicle. Driving force from the engine pushes a car forward, while gravity pulls it downwards and air resistance pushes against it. Traction is the friction created by a car's tyres and the ground, enabling the wheel to grip the road and move the car forward.

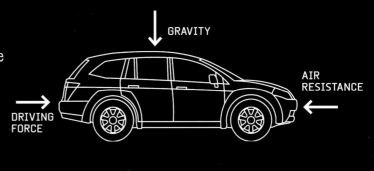

GRAVITY

AIR RESISTANCE

DRIVING FORCE

There are many areas of expertise required when designing a vehicle, requiring engineers and designers with specialist knowledge. Making a vehicle also involves several stages:

RESEARCH AND DEVELOPMENT

This stage is about finding solutions to engineering challenges, for example testing which vehicle shapes create the least air resistance, and researching what priorities customers are looking for in new models, for example affordability or power.

DESIGN

At this stage, the results of research and development are brought together by the designers who draw up the plans for new vehicle models.

PRODUCTION

The last stage is the planning and designing of the production process (how the vehicle will be put together in the factory), followed by the actual start of production itself.

THINKING OUTSIDE THE BOX!

Most vehicles stay in use for a long time. The average age of a car on the road in the USA is nearly 12 years, and the average age of a passenger aeroplane in the USA is 11 years. Due to the finite nature of fossil fuels (which currently power the majority of cars and planes), designers need to think now about how to power vehicles using renewable sources in the future (see pages 30–31).

Solar flying vehicles exist, such as the Helios prototype, but they cannot yet carry heavy goods and passengers.

LAND VEHICLES

MOST LAND VEHICLES USE WHEELS – EITHER TO RUN ALONG ROADS OR RAILS. THERE IS ARCHAEOLOGICAL EVIDENCE FOR WHEELED VEHICLES THAT DATES BACK NEARLY 6,000 YEARS. SEVERAL ANCIENT CULTURES IN THE MIDDLE EAST AND EUROPE APPEAR TO HAVE USED WHEELED VEHICLES AROUND 3,500 BCE. THESE EARLY LAND VEHICLES WERE WAGONS DESIGNED TO BE PULLED BY HUMANS OR ANIMALS.

A wheel is a circular object that spins around a fixed central bar, called an axle. Wheels on early vehicles were initially solid wooden circles, made of slices of tree trunk. In around 2000 BCE, the Egyptians developed the wheel further, cutting out holes to make the wheels lighter. The ancient Greeks added spokes for strength. Eventually fully spoked wheels were developed. These became common from 500 BCE onwards. Rubber tyres were added in the late 19th century to give a smoother ride. (See pages 32–33 for more on materials).

PROJECT

- Slide a book along a table with your hand. Now, place several straws or pencils in a row beneath the book, and slide it along the table again.

- Is it easier to slide the book with or without the straws or pencils?

- Which force is acting on the book, making it harder or easier to slide?

- Try this experiment on an uneven surface. Which is easier now? How could you move the book more easily over an uneven surface?

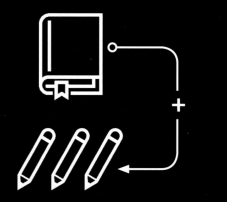

Some land vehicles don't have wheels, but use skis or tracks instead. On soft ground, such as sand or deep mud, wheels are ineffective because the small contact area between the vehicle and the ground creates an area of very high pressure. This can cause the vehicle to sink into the ground. A continuous track spreads the weight of the vehicle, meaning there is less pressure on the ground and the vehicle won't sink. Tracks also have a larger surface area than wheels, giving them better traction on slippery ground.

ENGINEERING TALK

The ridges on a track or tyre are known as its tread.

When designing tracked vehicles for slippery terrain, engineers look for ways to improve the traction even further. Rubber creates more traction on the ground than metal, but it is less hardwearing. So, engineers tend to use rubber tracks on lighter construction vehicles, but metal tracks on military or heavy equipment vehicles. Engineers can also increase the size of the tread to improve traction. Tread is the pattern of grooves and ridges on a track or a tyre. A large tread helps the track or tyre grip, particularly when moving over wet ground.

BICYCLES

THE FIRST TWO-WHEELED VEHICLE TO ACTUALLY BE GIVEN THE NAME 'BICYCLE' WAS THE PENNY FARTHING, INVENTED BY JAMES STARLEY IN 1870. IN THE LATE 19TH CENTURY, SEVERAL INVENTORS DEVELOPED DIFFERENT TYPES OF GEARS FOR BICYCLES, AND BY THE BEGINNING OF THE 20TH CENTURY, BICYCLES WERE MUCH LIKE THE ONES WE KNOW TODAY.

The Penny Farthing had pedals that turned the front wheel directly, and one wheel was much bigger than the other.

Bicycles are very popular due to their efficiency and relatively low cost. A survey of people in 44 different countries around the world showed that around 42 per cent of households own a bicycle. Modern bicycles are the most energy-efficient form of transport, converting around 90 per cent of energy supplied by the rider pedalling into energy moving the bicycle and rider forward.

THINKING OUTSIDE THE BOX!

In competitive cycling events such as the Tour de France, even the tiniest advantage over another rider can mean the difference between winning and losing. British cycling team, Team Sky, make tiny improvements that they call 'marginal gains'. They do things like testing the cyclists in a wind tunnel to improve aerodynamics, and even having all the cyclists bring pillows and bedding with them on tour so they can sleep in the same position every night!

Cyclists can make themselves more aerodynamic by leaning forwards.

TECHNOLOGY TALK

Gears are wheels with teeth that lock together. When one gear is turned, the gear it is connected to turns as well. Gears can be used to increase speed or increase force.

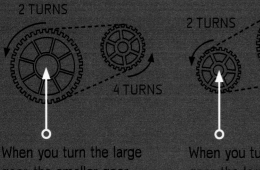

2 TURNS

4 TURNS

2 TURNS

1 TURN

When you turn the large gear, the smaller gear must turn faster to keep up with the larger one.

When you turn the small gear, the larger gear will turn more slowly, but with more force.

Gears help cyclists control their bicycles. Going up a hill, or getting a bicycle going from a standing start is hard work – it requires more force than keeping an already moving bicycle whizzing along. First gear on a bicycle transfers a high amount of force from the pedal to the rear wheel, making it easier to cycle up a hill or get a bike moving. But extra force comes at the expense of speed, as the rear wheel doesn't turn as far in first gear. Putting your bike into a higher gear means less force is transferred to the rear wheel, but it does turn a much greater distance. This is perfect for going at high speeds along flat roads.

CARS

IN 1885, GERMAN ENGINEER KARL BENZ BUILT THE FIRST MOTOR CAR WITH AN INTERNAL COMBUSTION ENGINE. IT HAD A TOP SPEED OF 16 KMPH. IN THOSE DAYS, MOTOR CARS WERE VERY EXPENSIVE AND RARE. BUT WHEN US INDUSTRIALIST HENRY FORD BROUGHT THE CAR INTO MASS PRODUCTION IN THE 20TH CENTURY, CAR OWNERSHIP BECAME POSSIBLE FOR THE AVERAGE PERSON IN A DEVELOPED NATION. TODAY, THERE ARE MORE THAN 1.2 BILLION CARS ON THE ROAD WORLDWIDE.

Most cars and trucks on the roads today still use an internal combustion engine, like the one in Karl Benz's first automobile. The internal combustion engine burns fuel, such as petrol, inside cylindrical chambers. Inside each cylinder is a piston, which is a metal disc on a rod. While the engine is running, fuel is mixed with air and ignited by an electric spark. The fuel and air explode and expand rapidly, forcing the pistons up and down within the cylinders. The piston rods are attached to a crankshaft which is rotated by the up and down movement of the pistons, in turn moving the wheels of the vehicle.

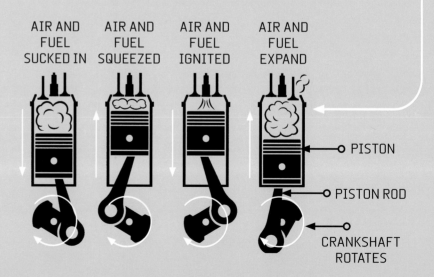

AIR AND FUEL SUCKED IN

AIR AND FUEL SQUEEZED

AIR AND FUEL IGNITED

AIR AND FUEL EXPAND

PISTON

PISTON ROD

CRANKSHAFT ROTATES

THINKING OUTSIDE THE BOX!

Almost all cars that have internal combustion engines run on one of two fuels: petrol or diesel. Diesel engines are more fuel-efficient than petrol engines, but they are also more harmful, releasing much more of the polluting gas nitrogen oxide than petrol engines do. Some car companies are researching using biofuels made from plants such as sugar cane or rapeseed, as these can produce less CO_2 than fossil fuels. However, biofuels have their own drawbacks as large amounts of land are required to grow the plants. (For more about alternative power sources, see pages 30–31).

In 1913 in the USA, industrialist Henry Ford introduced the assembly line. Instead of a team of people building a single car in one spot, each car was moved along a conveyor belt, with workers staying stationary. Starting with a bare chassis, the car moved along the production line, stopping to have parts added at each station. It was driven off the end of the line and the process only took 93 minutes from start to finish!

" ART TALK

Early cars were mostly owned by very wealthy people who often kept them as a hobby. The design of many early models reflected this, with luxury leather and velvet interiors, fine handcrafted parts and chrome and aluminium details. Some cars are still collectors' items, fetching high prices today. For example, a 1962 Ferrari 250 GTO sold at auction in 2014 for nearly US $35 million.

HALL OF FAME: CARS

THE INVENTION OF THE CAR HAD A MASSIVE IMPACT ON SOCIETY, CHANGING THE WAY WE LIVE AND WORK. DESIGNS HAVE EVOLVED SINCE THE EARLY 20TH CENTURY, REFLECTING CHANGING TASTES, NEEDS AND THE AVAILABLE TECHNOLOGY. CARS HAVE ALSO HAD AN IMPACT ON CULTURE, APPEARING IN MANY FILMS, AND BOOKS AND ON TV. HERE ARE SOME OF THE MOST ICONIC AND GROUND-BREAKING MODELS OF ALL TIME.

1880'S BENZ PATENT MOTORWAGEN

The first ever motor car with an internal combustion engine, the Benz Patent Motorwagen was invented by Karl Benz (see page 10). However, it was his wife, Bertha, who first drove it over a long distance. She made a 106 km trip with their two sons in 1888. Along the way, she had to solve many engineering challenges, for example when the brakes began to fail, she went to a cobbler to have leather pads fitted – thereby inventing the first brake pads.

1910'S FORD MODEL T

The Ford Model T was the first mass-produced car, outselling every other car on the market combined during its peak. It had a top speed of 70 kmph, and in 1913, one was produced every three minutes. The assembly line production technique influenced other areas of industry, as well as car design.

1930'S VOLKSWAGEN BEETLE

The Volkswagen Beetle was designed in the 1930s in Germany, in response to the need for a cheap mass-produced car for the country's new road network. The original Beetle only had a top speed of around 100 kmph but this popular basic design became the longest running and most-manufactured car of all time.

1980'S DELOREAN

Another cultural icon and an object of great desire for car fanatics in the 1980s was the DeLorean, made famous by the time-travel movie franchise *Back to the Future*. Featuring gull-wing doors and a brushed stainless-steel body, it had a very futuristic-looking style (for the time!).

2000'S TOYOTA PRIUS

In the 1990s, there was growing interest in hybrid cars (which combine electric and petrol engines), due to concerns around the price and availability of fossil fuels, as well as pollution and climate change. The Toyota Prius was released worldwide in 2000. It is still the top-selling hybrid car worldwide.

2010'S GOOGLE SELF-DRIVING WAYMO CAR

Not yet mainstream, this driverless car is believed by many to be the next step forward in human transportation. With sensors to detect objects and other road users, and an on-board navigation system, the Waymo car does not need a human to be in control of the vehicle.

MOTORBIKES

IN FILMS AND TV, THE MOTORBIKE HAS OFTEN HAD A GLAMOROUS ASSOCIATION WITH TOUGH, REBELLIOUS CHARACTERS. BUT FOR MANY PEOPLE AROUND THE WORLD, A MOTORBIKE IS THE ONLY FORM OF AFFORDABLE MOTORISED TRANSPORT.

Two German engineers, Hildebrand and Wolfmüller, invented the world's first mass-produced motorbike in 1894. It had a top speed of 45 kmph, and around 2,000 were made. But the high price and competition from other engineers meant the Hildebrand and Wolfmüller motorbike wasn't a commercial success. Motorbikes proved to be useful machines, however, and during the First World War (1914–1918), motorbike messengers replaced horse-backed dispatch riders.

ENGINEERING TALK

When you hear the word 'biker', the chances are you think of a pony-tailed dude, wearing heavy leathers, riding a 'chopper'. The original choppers in the 1960s and 1970s were motorbikes that had been re-engineered (or 'chopped') by motorbike enthusiasts at home, who were trying to improve standard models in terms of performance or visual appearance. For example, the forks that hold the front wheel were often lengthened, giving bikes a stretched-out look.

Today, motorbike sales are particularly high in some countries in Asia, where many people cannot afford a car, but a motorbike is within reach. In constant production since 1958, the Honda Super Cub is the most popular motorbike in the world, as its low price makes it competitive in many Asian markets. In the US and the UK, higher-end 'sport bikes' are popular with many motorbike enthusiasts. These types of motorbikes are optimised for high speed and handling over cost and fuel efficiency. They often have light, plastic bodywork and an aerodynamic riding position where the rider leans forward over the tank.

THINKING OUTSIDE THE BOX!

A popular use for motorbikes is motocross. Motocross is an off-road motorcycling sport, where competitors race around dirt tracks with hills, obstacles and jumps. Many tracks are in the countryside, where the loud engines of traditional petrol-powered bikes create a lot of noise pollution, annoying residents and disturbing the wildlife. Enter the electric motocross bike: a virtually silent alternative, pioneered by companies such as KTM and Zero. With developments in electric vehicle technology, electric motorbikes are finally beginning to be able to compete with the power of petrol-powered equivalents.

KTM Freeride EX 2017 motocross bike

LIGHTWEIGHT

DEEP TREAD FOR STRONG GRIP

TOUGH SUSPENSION

HIGH GROUND CLEARANCE

TRAINS

TRAINS ARE VEHICLES THAT RUN ALONG A FIXED TRACK. MODERN TRAINS ARE POWERED EITHER BY ELECTRICITY TAKEN FROM THE TRACK OR AN OVERHEAD WIRE, OR BY DIESEL ENGINES. THEY ARE A FAST AND EFFICIENT FORM OF OVERLAND TRAVEL.

In the 19th century, trains powered with steam engines revolutionised transport. Before the train, people's only option for long distance land travel was the stagecoach, which was slow and expensive. The new railways meant many people could be transported at a time, reducing the cost of long-distance travel and greatly increasing the speed. New rail networks linked cities in many countries. In America, railways enabled immigrants to settle new areas of the continent.

TECHNOLOGY TALK

Aside from a few tourist attractions, steam engines are no longer used for railways. However, steam turbine technology (heating water so it becomes steam and drives a machine in a rotating motion) is still very much in use today. In fact, it powers most of our homes and buildings! Steam turbines are used in the majority of electricity plants. Heat is produced by burning coal, through nuclear reactions or by geothermal energy from the Earth. This heat turns water into pressurised steam which drives turbines inside electricity generators, which in turn produce electrical energy.

Most modern high-speed trains are powered by electricity and run along rails. However, the fastest trains of all use maglev technology. Maglev trains levitate (hover) above the track using powerful electromagnets. This means there is no friction between the train and the track to slow it down. Maglevs are widely used in Japan where the current world speed record holder, the JR Central LO superconducting Maglev, has reached 603 kmph. They are also in use in China and Korea, and new tracks are proposed in Europe and the USA.

PROJECT

MAKE A MINI MAGLEV

Fix a row of flat magnets along the top of a wall of Lego® bricks to make the 'track'. Make sure all the magnets have the same pole facing upwards. Using sticky-tack, attach a couple of magnets to the underside of another Lego® piece to make the 'train'. Check that those magnets are the opposite way up to the ones on the wall, so that they repel each other. Add a vertical stabilising piece of Lego® either side of the 'train'. Place the train over the track.

- Does the train stay in place levitating over the rail?

- Do you need to add more weight to your train to make it sit at the right height over the track?

- How could your mini maglev be improved?

TRAIN

TRACK

STABILISER

WATER CRAFT

BEFORE THE INVENTION OF THE ROAD AND THE WHEEL, RIVERS WERE THE WORLD'S FIRST HIGHWAYS, WITH PEOPLE USING WATER CRAFT TO MOVE PEOPLE AND TRADE GOODS. THE WORLD'S OLDEST BOAT, A 10,000-YEAR-OLD DUGOUT CANOE, WAS FOUND IN A BOG IN THE NETHERLANDS.

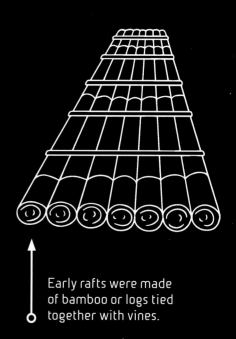

Early rafts were made of bamboo or logs tied together with vines.

The most basic water craft is a raft. This is a flat platform of buoyant materials that naturally float, such as wood. A boat, even a simple wooden canoe, is different from a raft in that it has a hull. This is the watertight body of the ship. A water craft with a hull is hollow on the inside. Boats come in a huge variety of different shapes, sizes and materials, but they all travel through the water by taking advantage of the same set of forces that enable them to float instead of sink (see Science Talk).

SCIENCE TALK

When you drop an object such as a coin into water, it pushes water out of the way to make space for itself. This is called displacement. An object will sink if it weighs more than the amount of water it has pushed out of the way. An object will float if it weighs less than the water it would have to push out of the way to make space for itself.

WEIGHT

BUOYANCY

CORK

IRON

Cork weighs less than water taking up the same amount of space, so it floats. Iron weighs more, so it sinks.

Even though boats can be very large and heavy, they are all hollow on the inside. There is air inside the boat below the water line which means that the overall weight of the boat, plus the air inside it, is less than the amount of water that would fill the same space. Extra weight in the bottom of the boat acts as 'ballast', which keeps the boat floating the right way up.

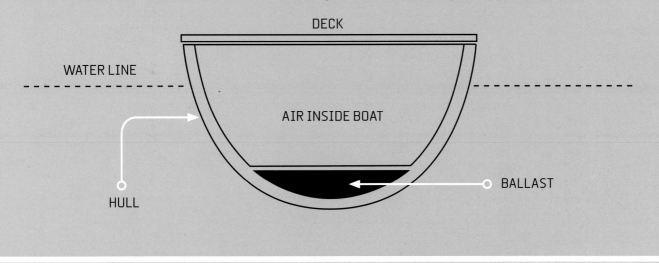

Not all water craft want to float – or at least not all the time! Submarines are designed to dive beneath the waves, and then rise back up to the surface by altering their buoyancy. To sink they pump water into special ballast tanks, making the craft heavier. To rise again, they push the water out of the tanks using pressurised air, making the craft lighter.

MATHS TALK

Deep under the ocean, the pressure is so great that if submarines were not specially constructed they would be crushed into a crumpled wreck. Pressure is measured in units called pascals. One kilo-pascal is the same as 1,000 pascals. One megapascal is equal to 1,000,000 pascals. The average pressure at sea level is around 101 kilo-pascals. The pressure at 10,000 metres below sea level (which is the depth the deepest submarine has dived to) is 110 megapascals. How many times greater is the pressure at 10,000 metres deep compared to at sea level?

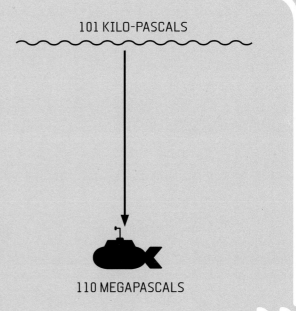

BOATS AND SHIPS

HUMANS HAVE USED BOATS AND SHIPS TO TRADE ACROSS THE OCEANS FOR CENTURIES, AND SHIPPING IS STILL HUGELY IMPORTANT TO THE WORLD ECONOMY TODAY. NINETY PER CENT OF GOODS TRADED INTERNATIONALLY ARE CARRIED BY SHIP.

Small boats can be powered by human energy, through rowing with oars. However, rowing is obviously not suitable for long journeys or for large, heavy ships. As long ago as 3500 BCE, the ancient Egyptians added cloth sails to their boats to capture energy from the wind. Wind was the main power source for ships and boats right up until the 19th century and the invention of steam power. Nowadays, the majority of ocean-going boats and ships are powered by combustion engines that burn fossil fuels.

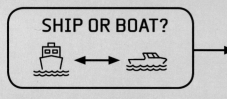

SHIP OR BOAT?

There is no strict definition of the difference between a boat and a ship. A rough distinction is that a ship could carry a boat (such as a large ship with lifeboats on board), but a boat cannot carry a ship.

PROJECT

Make a sail car out of a small cardboard box, cardboard wheels and skewers. Add the sails by sticking a skewer with a sail on vertically into the top of your car. Test out different sail designs and materials to find out which are the most efficient. Set up a testing area for your sail car, with a desk fan at one end, and a long area of flat ground in front of it.

■ How far and fast will your sail car on using different materials, sizes

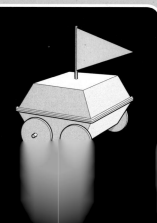

Ships are some of the largest vehicles on the planet. The 'Harmony of the Seas' is the largest cruise ship in the world. It is over 362 m long, which is longer than the Eiffel Tower is tall. It has many attractions on board, including an ice rink, a zip line and a theatre. Supertankers that carry raw materials and goods are also vast in length and can carry huge amounts of weight, some up to 657,000 tonnes!

Cargo ships carry goods around the world, however their engines are very polluting and are a significant contributor to climate change.

SCIENCE TALK

Large tankers that sail through deep water have huge propellers that spin and push the massive machines along. However, as propellers sit lower than the hull of the ship, they are not suitable for shallow water, where the blades might hit the seabed and break off. For vehicles such as jet skis or small motor boats that move in very shallow waters, impellers are better. These are propellers that are fitted within the main body of the boat. They suck water in through an inlet in the hull and push a jet of water out behind the craft, pushing it along.

JET SKI

HOVERCRAFT

HOVERCRAFT ARE STRANGE MACHINES – NOT QUITE A BOAT, NOT QUITE A PLANE, THEY CAN TRAVEL OVER WATER OR LAND, ALTHOUGH THEY TECHNICALLY MOVE THROUGH THE AIR! THIS VERSATILITY MAKES THEM VERY USEFUL.

Hovercraft can move seamlessly from land to water.

Hovercraft work by creating a cushion of air beneath the craft that they then float along on. This is achieved by having powerful downwards-facing fans underneath and in the centre of the craft which create a strong downdraught. This air is partially captured and turned into an air cushion by a flexible 'skirt' around the bottom edge of the craft. Other fans facing backwards then push the craft along and allow the captain to steer. Because a hovercraft floats above water, rather than moving through it, it hugely reduces water resistance, or drag.

HOW A HOVERCRAFT WORKS

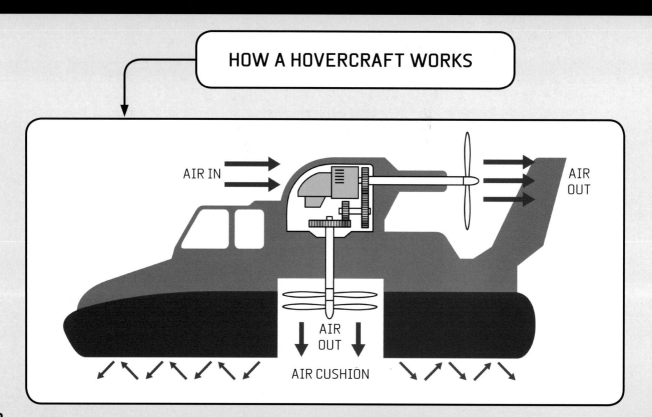

AIR IN

AIR OUT

AIR OUT

AIR CUSHION

"

MATHS TALK

The inventor of the hovercraft, Christopher Cockerell, discovered an interesting fact about them. The amount of weight a hovercraft can lift is proportional to the area of the air cushion (so, the amount of weight that can be carried increases with an increase in area of the air cushion). The energy required to create and contain the air cushion is proportional to the dimension of the skirt around the perimeter of the cushion.

Knowing these two facts, which of the two hovercraft below is less energy efficient? That is, which one needs more energy to lift each 100kg of weight?

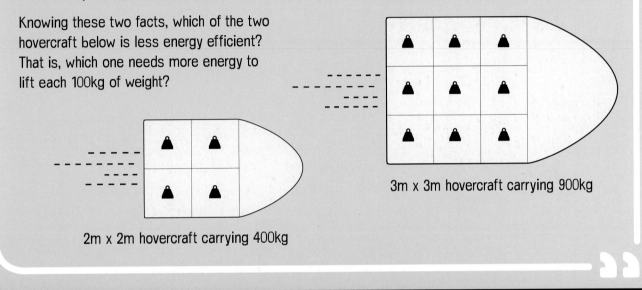

3m x 3m hovercraft carrying 900kg

2m x 2m hovercraft carrying 400kg

"

Hovercraft are great for difficult terrain. This is very useful in search and rescue scenarios. An emergency situation on an icy lake is a good example. A snowmobile can traverse thick ice but is a hazard on thin ice where it could break through. A hovercraft can easily transition between thick and thin or broken ice, without endangering the rescue team themselves.

THINKING OUTSIDE THE BOX!

Hovercraft also have commercial applications. Golf courses sometimes use hovercraft to spray fertiliser or spread grass seeds. This is because they can travel over waterlogged or freshly-laid grass without leaving track marks or damaging the ground.

AIRCRAFT

HUMANS HAVE DREAMT OF TAKING TO THE SKIES SINCE ANCIENT TIMES. THE GREAT ARTIST AND INVENTOR LEONARDO DA VINCI ATTEMPTED TO DESIGN FLYING MACHINES MODELLED ON BIRDS' WINGS IN THE 15TH CENTURY. HOWEVER, IT WASN'T UNTIL THE 18TH CENTURY THAT HUMANS MANAGED TO SUCCESSFULLY BUILD A FLYING VEHICLE.

Aircraft fall into three main types. First are craft that fly by being lighter than air. They include hot air balloons and airships. The second type of aircraft are those that use the laws of motion to generate lift, the force that lifts them into the air. These include aeroplanes and helicopters. A final type rely purely on thrust from a jet engine to move, such as a space rocket. These do not rely on the air to support them.

Jet engines push gases out behind them to move themselves along.

THINKING OUTSIDE THE BOX!

Most flying machines need power to generate lift and get off the ground. But once in the air, some aircraft are able to stay airborne and even gain height by taking advantage of weather phenomena. Gliders, light unpowered planes with broad wings, are able to soar on columns of rising air (thermals), much like birds of prey.

SILENT FLIERS

SCIENCE TALK

Hot air balloons and airships are able to fly in the same way that a boat is able to float. Hot air is less dense than the cold air in the atmosphere. Hydrogen or helium gas, which are used in airships, are also less dense than normal air. Because hot air is less dense, it weighs less than cold air. This means that a hot air balloon filled with hot air weighs less overall than the air around it — even including the basket and the passengers. So it rises up into the sky, much like a ball filled with air will rise up in water.

The French Mongolfier brothers developed a hot air balloon in the 18th century. The balloon was filled with hot air by burning straw in a pit below it. The very first manned flight (with a safe descent!) was in France in 1783, and hot air balloons and airships remained the only form of flying vessels until the 20th century. Modern hot air balloons use propane burners that blast hot air into the narrow end of the balloon.

Airships are filled with gases that are less dense than the surrounding air.

AEROPLANES

TODAY, WE CAN FLY FROM ONE SIDE OF THE WORLD TO THE OTHER IN LESS THAN A DAY. THERE ARE MORE THAN 3.5 BILLION JOURNEYS MADE BY AIR WORLDWIDE EACH YEAR. AS WELL AS CARRYING PASSENGERS, AEROPLANES ALSO PLAY AN IMPORTANT ROLE IN MOVING GOODS.

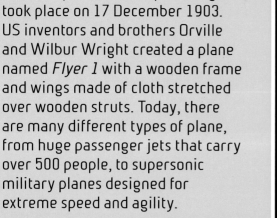

The first powered aeroplane flight took place on 17 December 1903. US inventors and brothers Orville and Wilbur Wright created a plane named *Flyer 1* with a wooden frame and wings made of cloth stretched over wooden struts. Today, there are many different types of plane, from huge passenger jets that carry over 500 people, to supersonic military planes designed for extreme speed and agility.

TECHNO TALK

The technology that most planes use to create lift is called an aerofoil. This basically describes the shape of a plane's wing. The wing is angled downwards and has a slight curve on the top. As the wing moves through the air, the air stream is split. The top half of the air stream follows the wing's curve, so as it leaves the rear edge of the wing, the air is angled downwards. This is called 'downwash'. This also affects the air stream below the wing, pushing it downwards. By pushing the air downwards, the wing is lifted up into the air.

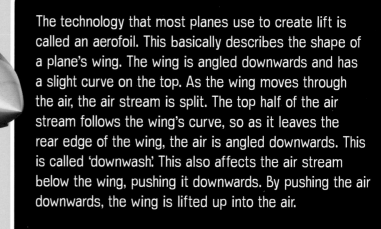

Air stream splits

Air is angled downwards

Wing (Aerofoil)

Wing is lifted up as air is pushed down

Airlines are always looking for ways to reduce costs. Planes run on fossil fuels, which are unsustainable, polluting and expensive. One way to make an aeroplane use less fuel is to make it lighter and cutting-edge materials technology is providing some solutions. 'Composites', which are high-tech plastics reinforced with carbon fibres, are 20-40 per cent lighter than metal, and are increasingly being used in passenger aircraft. Lightweight ceramics can be used for engine parts instead of metal alloys, while some airline companies are making their planes more aerodynamic by coating them in a clear acrylic to fill in any cracks or bumps. (For more on vehicle materials, see pages 32–33).

PROJECT

Make a paper aerofoil. Fold a piece of paper and tape the ends together. Carefully punch a hole through the front of the aerofoil, so that you can slide a cut-down drinking straw through it. Thread a piece of thin string or thread through the straw. Hold each end of the thread, so that it is taut and vertical, and run with it. The aerofoil should generate lift, and 'climb' up the thread.

■ How can you improve your aerofoil?

■ Does adding more of a curve to your aerofoil make a difference?

■ Could you make it from a different material?

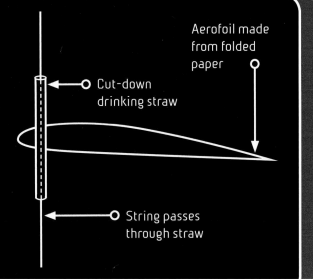

Aerofoil made from folded paper

Cut-down drinking straw

String passes through straw

HELICOPTERS

HELICOPTERS ALSO GENERATE LIFT WITH AEROFOILS, BUT INSTEAD OF FIXED WINGS, THEY HAVE SPINNING ROTOR BLADES. DURING THE EARLY 20TH CENTURY, MANY ENGINEERS AND INVENTORS EXPERIMENTED WITH MACHINES THAT RELIED ON ROTORS.

The blades of a helicopter create lift in the same way that an aeroplane's wings do. They also have an aerofoil shape, and as they move through the air, the air is forced downwards, pushing the helicopter upwards.

THINKING OUTSIDE THE BOX!

As helicopters are able to hover in place, and can fly forwards, backwards or sideways with a high level of accuracy, they are often used to pick up and put down cargo in the correct place, like a crane does. Special helicopters called Skycranes are used to perform tasks such as placing radio transmission towers high up on mountainsides, or in the logging industry to lift trees out of areas that ground vehicles cannot access.

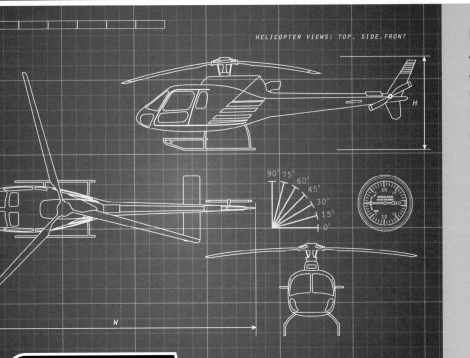

HELICOPTER VIEWS: TOP, SIDE, FRONT

90° 75° 60° 45° 30° 15° 0°

Helicopters have an advantage over fixed wing aircraft in that they can take off and land vertically. This enables them to be used in places where an aeroplane would be unable to land, such as on the tops of buildings or on roads. As well as offering vertical take-off and landing, being able to hover in place in the air makes them useful for tasks such as search and rescue, aerial surveys and patrols.

PROJECT

Make a paper rotocopter using the template below. Cut along the solid lines and then fold along the dotted lines, so you create a mini paper rotocopter like the picture. Slide a paperclip on the bottom to add weight.

- Drop the paper rotocopter from a height. What happens?

- What happens when you add more weight?

- Does altering the length or angles of the blades at the top have an effect?

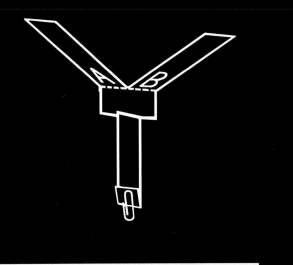

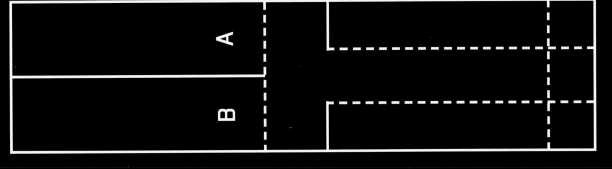

POWER

OVER THE COURSE OF HISTORY, WE HAVE POWERED OUR VEHICLES IN VARIOUS DIFFERENT WAYS, FROM OARS TO HORSES, WIND, STEAM, PETROL OR DIESEL. IN THE FUTURE, IT IS LIKELY THAT ELECTRIC-POWERED VEHICLES MAY BECOME THE NORM.

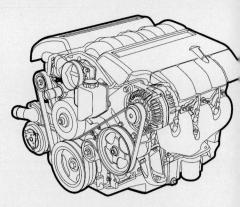

Engines have become more powerful over time, but the next goal is being eco-friendly, too.

Most vehicles are still powered by burning fuels – mostly fossil fuels, in an internal combustion engine. There are various different fossil fuels including petrol, diesel and liquid petroleum gas – but there are all made from the same stuff: crude oil. One problem with fossil fuels is that they are finite – they will one day run out. Burning fossil fuels also creates a lot of pollution. It releases toxic gases into the air, which kill millions of people around the world each year and are a main contributor to climate change (see Science Talk).

SCIENCE TALK

The most significant problem caused by burning fossil fuels is the resulting huge release of carbon dioxide into the atmosphere. The increase of CO^2 in the Earth's atmosphere is contributing to climate change. This disrupts weather patterns around the world, causing areas of drought, as well as super storms and dangerous flooding. The effects of extreme weather and drought-related food shortages can be deadly.

As an alternative to vehicles that rely on fossil fuels, electric cars are slowly becoming more popular. They are more energy-efficient, less polluting and are quieter, but a downside is that they can take a long time to charge. Electric vehicles can be recharged overnight at home using mains electricity. Rapid chargers are also available at some service stations, giving a partial charge in only half an hour. However, in order to be genuinely environmentally friendly, the electricity itself must be generated by renewable means, such as by wind turbines or solar farms.

THINKING OUTSIDE THE BOX!

Some large ships and submarines are powered by nuclear reactors, which release energy by splitting atoms apart. Nuclear reactors do not need air to burn their fuel, which makes them very useful for powering submarines underwater. Nuclear energy is incredibly powerful and efficient, so vehicles can travel vast distances without needing to stop and refuel. The ten *Nimitz*-class US Aircraft Carriers are powered by two nuclear reactors that enable them to operate for 20 years without refuelling.

MATERIALS

VEHICLE MATERIALS HAVE CHANGED OVER TIME. IN THE PAST, CARTS AND SHIPS WERE MADE MAINLY OF WOOD. IN THE STEAM AGE OF THE 19TH CENTURY, IRON AND STEEL BECAME THE MATERIALS OF CHOICE. ALUMINIUM, WHICH IS LIGHTER, CAME INTO HIGH DEMAND FOR AEROPLANE BUILDING DURING THE FIRST WORLD WAR. MODERN MATERIALS INCLUDE NEW TYPES OF METAL AND CARBON FIBRE.

Vehicles need to move, so they must be light in order to be fuel-efficient, but they also need to be strong. Price and visual appearance (aesthetics) also need to be taken into account when choosing the right materials. Today, cars are mostly made of a mixture of steel, aluminium and plastic. Steel is normally used for the body, which needs to be strong. To reduce weight, the bonnet and sometimes the side panels are made of aluminium as it is a lighter metal.

STRENGTH Vs SPEED

Elephants are heavy and comparatively slow, but are incredibly strong.

The cheetah is light, fast and agile, but not as strong as the elephant.

THINKING OUTSIDE THE BOX!

Engineers are looking at a new material that can be a real winner in terms of price, aesthetics and sustainability... bamboo. Treated with a special coating, bamboo is already being used in bicycles and even for small cars. It is amazingly cheap and renewable, as some species of bamboo grow at a rate of up to one metre per day!

Materials scientists are making amazing developments with light, strong materials, working at the level of individual molecules, the tiny building blocks that make up all stuff. Materials made of carbon nanotubes – tiny tubes of carbon only one molecule thick – have the potential to be unbelievably light and strong.

PROJECT

Test how the structure of a material makes a difference to its strength. Fill a plastic cup with coins to create a weight. Give it a long, looped handle made of string by punching two holes in either side of the cup. Using multiple sheets of origami paper, can you create an object that the cup can hang from without creasing or bending the paper?

- Do tube shapes work?

- Can you weave the paper together in any way and what effect does this have?

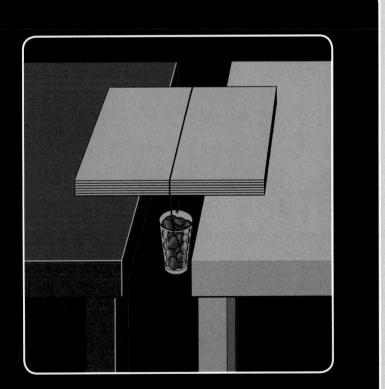

SPEED

PEOPLE JUST SEEM TO HAVE A NEED FOR SPEED! WHEN THE STEAM TRAIN WAS FIRST INVENTED, PEOPLE THOUGHT THAT GOING AT PREVIOUSLY UNIMAGINABLE SPEEDS OF AROUND 50 KMPH WOULD HAVE SERIOUS NEGATIVE HEALTH EFFECTS, SUCH AS MAKING PEOPLE UNABLE TO BREATHE OR DAMAGING THEIR EYES. WE NOW REGULARLY TRAVEL AT MUCH FASTER SPEEDS – BUT ENGINEERS ARE STILL LOOKING TO GO EVEN FASTER.

Air resistance is one of the strongest forces acting against moving vehicles. The faster you travel, the stronger the air resistance becomes. Aerodynamics is the science of how to move through the air as efficiently as possible to reduce air resistance. Using streamlined (thin, pointy) shapes is key to making a vehicle as aerodynamic as possible.

ENGINEERING TALK

Engineers use wind tunnels to test the aerodynamics of new vehicles. These are large buildings that contain giant fans to blow air at high speeds. This replicates the effect of a vehicle moving along at high speed. Engineers can then use coloured smoke, air-speed measuring instruments, or special photography that can detect air pressure to see how the air is moving around the vehicle.

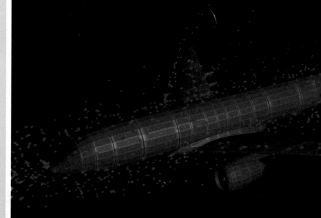

As well as being the best, most aerodynamic shape possible, a vehicle designed to break speed records needs to be powerful. The current land speed record is held by the Thrust SSC, which is a supersonic car powered by two large jet engines. It reached 1,228 kmph in October 1997, becoming the first land vehicle to break the sound barrier.

SCIENCE TALK

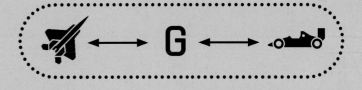

Although people in the 19th century were wrong about the dangers of travelling at 50 kmph, rapidly increasing speed can have negative effects on the body. Ever been on a rollercoaster and felt like your body was being almost squashed by the movement? That's g-force. G-force acts on objects (and humans) during rapid acceleration, deceleration (see page 36) or directional change. Racing car drivers, jet plane pilots and astronauts all experience powerful g-forces, which they have to train to get used to. People experiencing high g-forces when they aren't used to it can pass out, or have temporary loss of vision.

BRAKING

AS WELL AS MOVING FORWARD, VEHICLES ALSO NEED TO STOP SAFELY. TO DO THIS, VEHICLES MUST GENERATE FORCES THAT COUNTERACT THEIR FORWARD MOTION. BRAKES ON WHEELED VEHICLES TEND TO USE FRICTION. AEROPLANES ALSO MAKE USE OF AIR RESISTANCE.

Bicycles usually have rim brakes. Two rubber pads sit on either side of the wheel, and squeeze against the metal rim to slow the bike down. Cars have disc brakes or drum brakes. Disc brakes work a bit like rim brakes, but instead of the two brake pads squeezing the wheel itself, they squeeze a disc attached to the wheel. Drum brakes have two curved brake pads that sit inside the wheel itself, and push out against its inner surface.

DISC

WHEEL HUB (WHEEL REMOVED)

BRAKE PADS SQUEEZE DISC

MATHS TALK

Acceleration equals the change in speed divided by the time taken.

In normal life, we use the term deceleration to talk about slowing down, but in science they use positive and negative acceleration.

So, negative acceleration means that something has slowed down (decelerated). If a car decreases its speed from 25 metres a second to 15 metres a second in 5 seconds, what is its acceleration?

The change in speed is the end speed minus the start speed, so the change in speed for our car is: $15 - 25 = -10$ m/s

Therefore, the acceleration can be worked out like this: $-10 \div 5 = ?$

Passenger jets need to decelerate very rapidly. If pilots tried to do this by braking using the wheels alone, the wheels would melt, due to the heat caused by the friction of the brakes on the wheels. So, they also use reverse thrust, where they change the engines to push the exhaust gases out forwards, rather than backwards, to slow the plane. They also raise spoilers on a plane's wings to create additional air resistance and reduce lift.

SPOILERS decrease lift and create drag, helping to slow the plane down.

FLAPS create drag, also slowing the plane down.

THINKING OUTSIDE THE BOX!

Super-fast land vehicles pose an engineering challenge, as they can move at speeds where brakes could melt or cause skidding, but they have no wings to place spoilers on and increase drag. A solution here is to use parachutes. These slow the descent of a falling object and can also provide a braking system for fast land vehicles. Parachutes were used on the back of the Thrust SSC (see page 35).

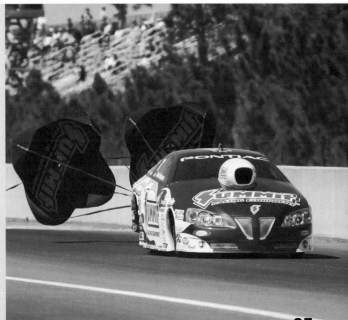

SAFETY FEATURES

HUMANS ARE SOFT, SQUISHY CREATURES, AND MOVING AROUND IN METAL OBJECTS AT HIGH SPEEDS IS QUITE DANGEROUS. AN AVERAGE OF 1.3 MILLION PEOPLE DIE IN CAR CRASHES EVERY YEAR WORLDWIDE, WITH AN ADDITIONAL 20-50 MILLION INJURED OR DISABLED.

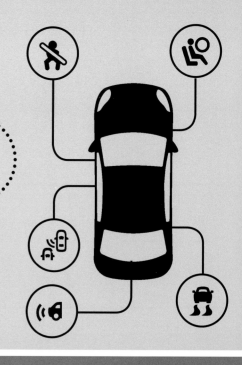

When a car is involved in a collision, the powerful forces involved can cause injury. Modern vehicles are now fitted with many safety features. Seat belts stop passengers from being flung forward and through the windscreen due to the rapid deceleration. Airbags cushion a passenger if they are flung forward, and can help prevent cuts from broken glass. Safety cages are strong, steel cages that strengthen the area where passengers sit to keep them safe.

SCIENCE TALK

An object in motion will keep moving unless another force is applied to it. This is called momentum. A car in motion has a lot of momentum. In the event of a collision, the car will decelerate rapidly. Unsecured objects and people inside the car continue forward at their previous speed, and will hit the vehicle's interior with a force many times their normal weight, due to momentum. Crumple zones are areas at the front of the car that are designed to absorb energy during a collision to help reduce the difference in speed between the vehicle and the occupants.

Engineers model and test the safety features of cars in various ways. They can use advanced computer modelling to test out the crashworthiness of cars at the design stage. Car makers also carry out crash tests – destructive testing where cars are impacted onto a solid concrete wall at a specified speed.

PROJECT

Try this egg drop experiment. Using various materials, such as straws, lolly sticks, paper, tape, plastic bags, plastic containers and so on – can you create a system that will stop an egg from breaking when it is dropped onto a hard floor from a one metre height?

■ How can you make the egg decelerate more slowly on impact?

■ Which materials work best?

Crash test dummies are used to mimic the movement of a human body during a car crash.

STYLE

PEOPLE USE VEHICLES TO GET FROM A TO B, BUT THEY HAVE MORE THAN JUST A PRACTICAL USE. CARS, BIKES AND BOATS CAN ALSO BE A STATUS SYMBOL. PEOPLE WANT THEIR VEHICLES TO LOOK GOOD!

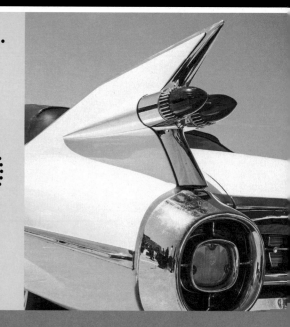

Even the basic shape of a car is affected by fashion. During the 1950s, the world was obsessed by everything Space Age, as the USA and the Soviet Union competed to be the first superpower to put someone in space. Spacecraft influenced car design in the 1950s and 1960s, with cool tail fins, such as on the Cadillac Eldorado. In the mid-1970s and 1980s, angular wedge designs were popular, such as the Lamborghini Countach. Today, cars come in many different shapes, but a lot of brands are referencing classic designs from history, updated with new technology.

" ART TALK

As well as the overall shape of the vehicle, different colours and paint jobs come in and out of fashion, as new technology is developed and depending on what is in style at the time. In the 1960s, racing stripes, also called 'go faster stripes', would sometimes be painted on road cars as a decorative detail. New paint technology means some cars now have chameleon paint which changes colour according to the angle of view and lighting.

This car has paint that is either purple or blue depending on the angle you are viewing it from.

For the super wealthy, personalised designs are a must-have. Enter the world of custom-designed yachts and private planes. Companies can help billionaires create completely personalised interiors for their private vehicles, with ultra-high end stylings such as marble bathrooms with solid gold fixtures and fittings!

A luxury yacht can be a fabulous home on the water. Some have cinemas and swimming pools on board!

PROJECT

Design a car to your own personal taste.

- What shape would it be?
- What colour would it be?
- What detailing will you give it?

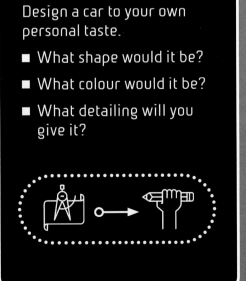

IF THERE IS A RECORD, THE CHANCES ARE AN ENGINEER OR A SCIENTIST SOMEWHERE IS TRYING TO FIGURE OUT HOW TO BREAK IT! HERE ARE SOME OF THE MOST AMAZING VEHICLE WORLD RECORDS.

FASTEST ELECTRIC CAR

The NIO EP9 is a double world record-holder. In May 2017, it set the record lap time for an electric car at the 20.8 kilometre Nürburgring in Germany, racing around in only 6 minutes and 46 seconds. In February 2017, it also set an additional world record: the fastest autonomous (driverless) electric car in the world. The car drove around the 5.5-kilometre-long Circuit of the Americas track in Texas in 2 minutes and 40.33 seconds, driven entirely by software.

CHEAPEST CAR

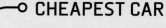

Launched in India in 2008, the Nano was designed by Indian company Tata to offer an alternative to motorbike ownership. It is very basic, with no airbags, and the boot is only accessible from inside the car. The initial cost was only 10,000 rupees, or about $1,500 dollars.

FURTHEST HUMAN-POWERED FLIGHT

Creating an aeroplane that can take off and fly under human power alone is a significant engineering challenge due to the high power to weight ratio. Some early, very short straight flights were achieved as early as 1961. The current distance record was set by the MIT Daedalus 88. It flew 115.11 kilometres in 3 hours and 54 minutes in April 1988.

LARGEST AIRCRAFT

Airships might not have a very futuristic reputation, but the *Airlander 10* is a ground-breaker in several ways. It is a hybrid airship, meaning it relies on both the lift generated by the lighter-than-air gas inside, as well as the lift created by the aerofoil-type shape of the contoured and flattened hull as it moves through the air. At 92 m long and 43.5 m wide it is the largest aircraft in the world. It completed its first series of test flights in 2016.

MOST POWERFUL ROCKET

NASA is currently developing the most powerful rocket in the world, the Space Launch System, or SLS. The SLS' first, unmanned test flight is scheduled for 2019. This incredibly powerful rocket will be capable of going further than any rocket has been before, reaching deep space (the furthest reaches of our solar system, and beyond). It will also be used for a two-year long manned mission to Mars, currently scheduled for 2033.

LARGEST SOLAR POWERED BOAT

The Tûranor PlanetSolar is another double world record-holder. It is the largest solar-powered boat in the world, at 31 m long and is covered by 537 m² of solar panels. Inside the ship's twin hulls are 8.5 tons of lithium ion batteries to store the electrical energy produced by the solar panels. It became the first ever entirely solar-powered vehicle to circumnavigate the Earth in May 2012.

VEHICLES OF THE FUTURE

OVER THE NEXT 50 TO 100 YEARS, WE WILL LIKELY SEE HUGE CHANGES IN VEHICLE DESIGN, AS ENGINEERS MUST ADAPT VEHICLES FOR CHALLENGES SUCH AS THE LACK OF FOSSIL FUELS AND OVERPOPULATION IN CITIES. IMPROVEMENTS IN TECHNOLOGY WILL ALSO CHANGE THE WAY WE INTERACT WITH VEHICLES.

Air traffic is set to increase seven-fold by 2050, and despite technological improvements and updated air fleets which should stop CO_2 emissions from rising at exactly the same rate, emissions will still increase four-fold unless significant changes are made. Aeroplanes are some of the most damaging CO_2 emitters as they put it straight into the high atmosphere. Some scientists predict that electric planes will be available by 2050. NASA is currently building experimental electric planes, such as the *X-57 Maxwell*, which will be powered only by batteries.

The *X-57 Maxwell* is electric, but currently can only carry two people, and has a maximum flight time of one hour.

TECHNO TALK

The key technology that needs to be improved for electric planes to become a reality is battery technology. At the moment, batteries are not energy-dense enough to power planes for long distances or high speeds. However, due to the high potential rewards of improved battery technology, many companies and organisations around the world are working hard to develop the next battery technology breakthrough.

Self-driving cars are also likely to revolutionise the way we travel in future. The Google Waymo car (see page 13) is one of the most advanced autonomous vehicles being developed today. The car senses its surroundings with a high-tech LiDAR system: lasers are bounced off the surrounding objects to detect how far away they are, while radar helps sense objects in snow, rain and fog. Some cars on the road today already use similar technology to park autonomously, without the driver being in control.

THINKING OUTSIDE THE BOX!

As cities become more and more heavily populated, it will become less and less economical to own private cars or transport. Experts predict that in the future there will be fleets of small, self-driving vehicles that can whizz around a city to collect and move passengers at the touch of an app, a bit like Uber.

GLOSSARY

aerodynamics the science of how air moves around moving objects

aesthetics the look of an object, such as the shape, form, colour and style

autonomous vehicle a vehicle that is capable of sensing its environment and navigating itself

biofuel a fuel manufactured from plants or animal waste

buoyant materials that float

chassis the basic frame of a car

chopper originally a motorbike that had been adapted at home by a motorbike enthusiast, later a term to describe motorbikes that had a 'stretched' appearance and a laid-back riding position

collision a crash

finite a limited amount, meaning it will run out

fossil fuel a fuel such as coal or oil, which formed underground from plant and animal remains over millions of years

friction a force created when surfaces rub against one another

hybrid a vehicle that uses a mixture of fossil fuels and electricity for power

lift a force that opposes the weight of an airborne vehicle and keeps it in the air

Maglev a system where trains hover above a track, supported by magnetic repulsion

momentum the tendency of a moving object to continue moving

spoiler a flap on a car or aeroplane that disrupts the airflow around the vehicle to change the amount of air resistance or lift being created

stagecoach a horse-drawn carriage

suspension a set of parts in a vehicle that help reduce the jolting effect of travelling over dips and bumps in the road

sustainable able to be maintained without using up natural resources or harming the environment

terrain the type of ground

thrust the propelling force created by a jet or rocket engine

traction a force that causes a moving thing to stick to the surface it is moving along

tread The ridges on a tyre or continuous track that help the vehicle grip the ground

turbine a fan-like machine that spins in a flow of water or steam to generate power

velocipede An early form of bicycle propelled by the rider's feet pushing on the ground, similar to a modern children's balance bike

FURTHER READING

Machines and Vehicles: The World in Infographics Jon Richards (Wayland, 2014)

Motorbikes: Ultimate Machines Rob Scott Coulson (Wayland, 2013)

The Story of the Car Giles Chapman (Wren & Rook, 2017)

WEBSITES

FIND OUT MORE ABOUT VEHICLES AT THE FOLLOWING WEBSITES

www.explainthatstuff.com/articles_transportation.html

www.sciencekids.co.nz/sciencefacts/vehicles.html

www.ltmcollection.org/vehicles/index.html

QUIZ

- Which force helps a vehicle's tyre or track to grip the ground?
- Who built the first motor car?
- How were the first trains powered?
- How do engineers test a vehicle's aerodynamics?
- Name three types of brake.

INDEX

QUIZ ANSWERS

- Traction
- Karl Benz
- The first trains were steam powered.
- Using a wind tunnel
- Rim brakes, disc brakes and drum brakes

BUILDINGS

- Starting out ▪ Materials
- Structure ▪ Arches and domes
- Designing a building ▪ Scale and plans ▪ Perspective ▪ Ancient buildings ▪ Greeks and Romans
- Castles and cathedrals ▪ Architects
- Houses ▪ Eco-friendly buildings
- Skyscrapers ▪ Landmarks
- Public buildings ▪ Bridges
- Famous bridges ▪ Tunnels
- When things go wrong
- Hostile conditions

COMPUTERS

- A Computer is... ▪ Computers everywhere ▪ Ones and zeros
- A computer's brain ▪ Memory
- Inputs ▪ Outputs ▪ Programming
- Early days ▪ Computer scientists
- Software ▪ Graphics ▪ Games
- Personal computers ▪ Networks
- The web ▪ Virtual reality
- Artificial intelligence ▪ Amazing computers ▪ A changed planet
- Future computers

MATERIALS

- Choosing Materials ▪ Natural or Manmade ▪ Solid ▪ Liquid ▪ Gas
- Rocks and Minerals ▪ Wood
- Metal ▪ Glass ▪ Building
- Plastics ▪ Ceramics ▪ Textiles
- Art ▪ Composites ▪ Chemicals
- Super Materials ▪ Special Surfaces
- Shape Changers ▪ Recycling
- Future Materials

ROBOTS

- Designing a robot ▪ Moving parts
- Circuits ▪ Sensors ▪ Sight and navigation ▪ Code ▪ Programming robots ▪ Artificial intelligence
- Robot ethics ▪ The first robots
- Robots in danger ▪ Robots in space
- Drones and cars ▪ Real robots
- Household robots ▪ Robots and medicine ▪ Bionics ▪ Robotic arms
- Androids ▪ Fictional robots

SPACE

- Learning about space ▪ Our solar system ▪ Stars ▪ Galaxies and the universe ▪ Comets and meteors
- Black holes ▪ The Big Bang
- Astronomers ▪ Observatories and telescopes ▪ Space exploration
- The science of space ▪ Astronauts
- Training for space
- The International Space Station
- Space walks ▪ Rockets ▪ Rovers
- Space probes ▪ Satellites
- Space colonies ▪ Future exploration

VEHICLES

- Designing a vehicle ▪ Land vehicles ▪ Bicycles ▪ Cars
- Famous cars ▪ Trains ▪ Watercraft
- Boats and ships ▪ Hovercraft
- Aircraft ▪ Aeroplanes
- Helicopters ▪ Extreme terrain vehicles ▪ Power ▪ Materials
- Speed ▪ Braking ▪ Safety features
- Style ▪ Record breakers
- Vehicles of the future